The 3-D Library of the Human Body

THE MOUTH AND NOSE

LEARNING HOW WE TASTE AND SMELL

Jennifer Viegas

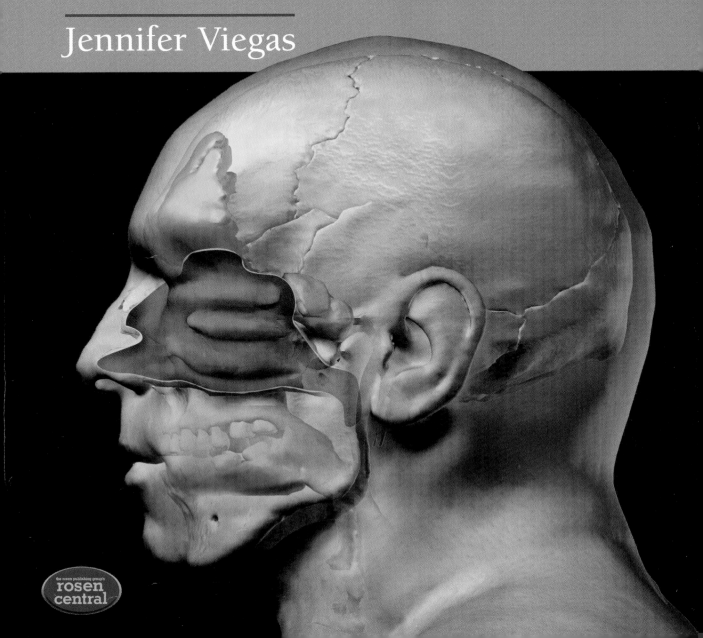

the rosen publishing group's
rosen
central

Editor's Note

The idea for the illustrations in this book originated in 1986 with the Vesalius Project at Colorado State University's Department of Anatomy and Neurobiology. There, a team of scientists and illustrators dreamed of turning conventional two-dimensional anatomical illustrations into three-dimensional computer images that could be rotated and viewed from any angle, for the benefit of students of medicine and biology. In 1988 this dream became the Visible Human Project™, under the sponsorship of the National Library of Medicine in Bethesda, Maryland. A grant was awarded to the University of Colorado School of Medicine, and in 1993 the first work of dissection and scanning began on the body of a Texas convict who had been executed by lethal injection. The process was repeated on the body of a Maryland woman who had died of a heart attack. Applying the latest techniques of computer graphics, the scientific team was able to create a series of three-dimensional digital images of the human body so beautiful and startlingly accurate that they seem more in the realm of art than science. On the computer screen, muscles, bones, and organs of the body can be turned and viewed from any angle, and layers of tissue can be electronically peeled away to reveal what lies underneath. In reproducing these digital images in two-dimensional print form, the editors at Rosen have tried to preserve the three-dimensional character of the work by showing organs of the body from different perspectives and using illustrations that progressively reveal deeper layers of anatomical structure.

Published in 2002 by The Rosen Publishing Group, Inc.
29 East 21st Street, New York, NY 10010

Digital anatomy images published by arrangement with Anatographica, LLC.
216 East 49th Street, New York, NY 10017

First Edition

Library of Congress Cataloging-in-Publication Data

Viegas, Jennifer.
The mouth and nose: learning how we taste and smell / Jennifer Viegas. — 1st ed.
p. cm. — (The 3-D library of the human body)
Includes bibliographical references and index.
Summary: Discusses the anatomy and physiology of the mouth and nose and explains how these sensory organs enable us to taste and smell.
ISBN 0-8239-3535-3
1. Mouth—Juvenile literature. 2. Nose—Juvenile literature. 3. Taste—Juvenile literature. 4. Smell—Juvenile literature. [1. Mouth. 2. Nose. 3. Taste. 4. Smell. 5. Senses and sensations.]
I. Title. II. Series.
QP146 .V54 2001
612.8'6—dc21

2001002889

Manufactured in the United States of America

CONTENTS

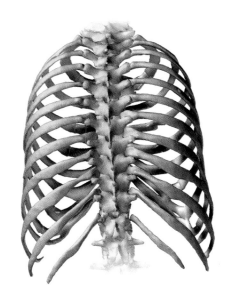

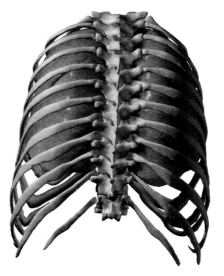

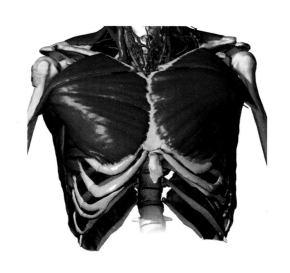

PREFACE
A BRIEF HISTORY OF ANATOMICAL ILLUSTRATION

The science of anatomy can be traced back to ancient Egyptian and Chinese civilizations, and was very well advanced by the time of the establishment of the medical schools of ancient Alexandria, around 300 BC. This knowledge was further advanced during Roman times, especially by a Greek doctor named Galen, who lived from about AD 130 to AD 200. With the collapse of the Roman Empire, much of this knowledge was lost to the West, but it was preserved by Arab scholars during Europe's Dark Ages and again became available in Europe during the Middle Ages and the Renaissance. Medical schools appeared in Italy and France in the thirteenth century, and by the fifteenth century, these schools were producing illustrated anatomy texts.

The problem for Renaissance scholars was that they were trying to produce accurate drawings of the human body and also to reestablish the authority of the ancient Greeks and Romans. But even some of Galen's ideas about human anatomy were wrong, and the attempt to reconcile his work with what was really known about the body created problems, even in the work of the greatest artist of the human form, Leonardo da Vinci. In 1543, a contemporary of da Vinci's, Andreas Vesalius, published *De Humani Corporis Fabrica* (On the structure of the human body), the first anatomy text to break with ancient authorities and present accurate human anatomy based purely on scientific observation. Vesalius's work is considered a great landmark in the history of medical science. His illustrations were printed from carved woodcuts.

The early nineteenth century saw the development of new techniques for color printing, and by the 1830s, anatomy texts featured large color plates. One of the landmarks of this period was *Anatomy Descriptive and Surgical* by Henry Gray, published in 1858. Gray's *Anatomy* has been revised and reprinted many times in the last 140 years, but it presents idealized forms for teaching purposes. Only with the development of photographic printing could anatomy books present the human body the way it would actually be seen on the dissecting table by medical students, with all its individual imperfections.

In the twentieth century, a whole range of new techniques enabled medical illustrators to improve their work: X rays, endoscopy, CAT and MRI scanning, and finally digital imaging, which is the technique used for the illustrations in this book. With digital imaging, the true three-dimensional shape of the human body is preserved in electronic form, and almost any view or perspective can be selected for printing. Digital imaging is the last word in accurate anatomical illustration, as one can see from the marvelous reproductions in the 3-D Library of the Human Body.

1
THE JAW, MOUTH, AND THROAT

The human skull is familiar to most people, either from reproductions in museums or models used as decorations around Halloween time. These models usually are lightweight, but real human heads on average weigh 8.8 pounds. That is like carrying a bowling ball on your shoulders all day and night. Thankfully, strong bones and muscles in the neck hold up the head.

The skeleton part of the head, called the skull, functions like a box made of bones. It holds and protects all of the important organs located in the head. These include the brain, ears, eyes, nose, and mouth.

While the skull looks like one big bone, it actually consists of twenty-nine separate bones. The section of bone encasing the brain is called the cranium, which is made up of eight connected bones. Fourteen interlocking bones frame the nose, mouth, and eyes. The hole where the nose is located reveals how air can enter the body.

The Jaw

The jaw has an upper and lower section. The upper jaw, called the maxilla, consists of two bones. The lower jaw, referred to as the mandible, is hinged where it meets the upper jaw. This enables the mandible to move up and down, while the top part of the jaw stays relatively still. To get an idea of how this works, stretch out all of the fingers of one hand, except the thumb. Next, move the thumb up and down. Here the fingers work like the maxilla and the thumb acts as the mandible.

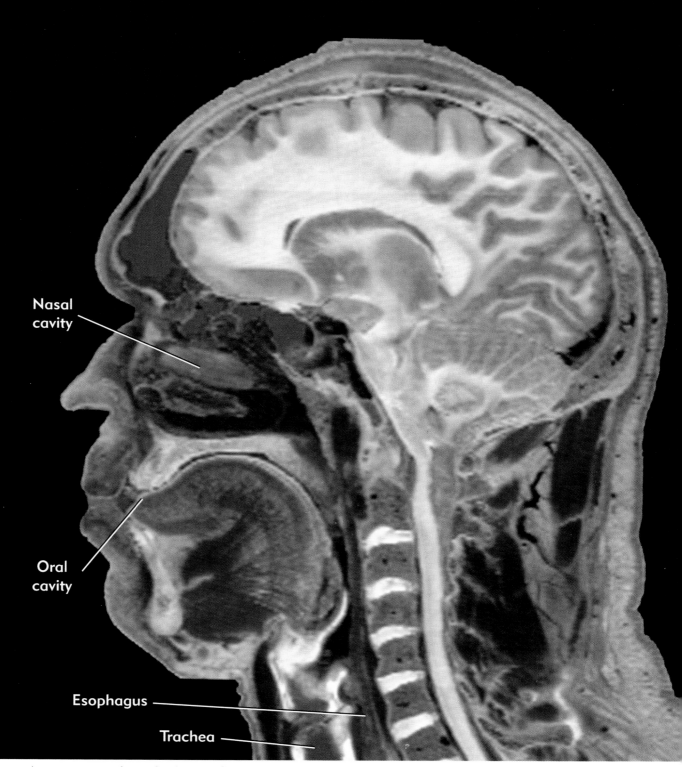

Nasal
cavity

Oral
cavity

Esophagus

Trachea

A cross-sectional view of the head and neck. The mouth and nasal cavities are visible, as is the esophagus and the trachea, or windpipe.

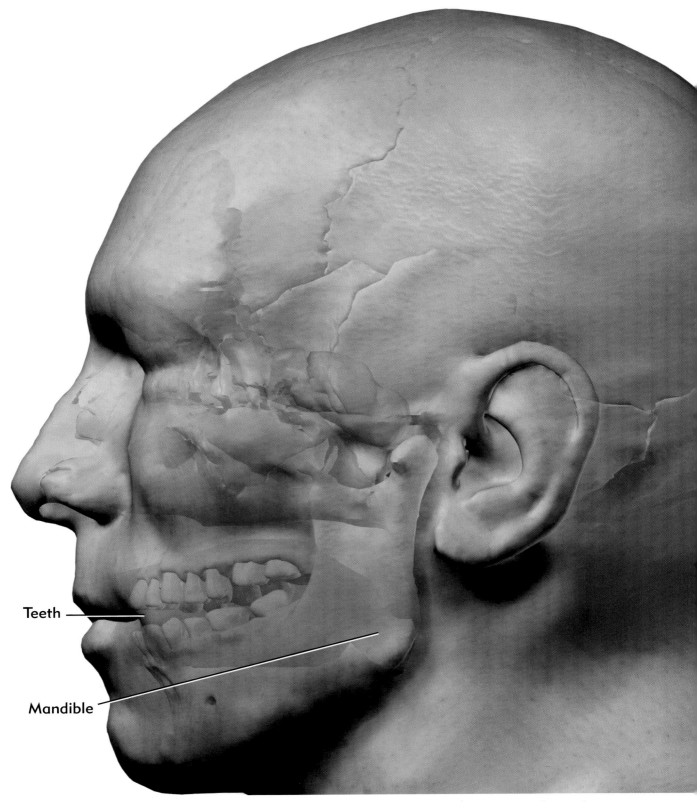

Teeth ——————

Mandible ——————

This lateral, or side, view of the head shows the jawbone and teeth. The jawbone, or mandible, is controlled by some of the most powerful muscles in the body.

Muscles stretching from the neck to the top of the head help to close the lower jaw. These muscles are incredibly strong. They allow the jaw to close with a force of 200 pounds! Such strength gives the jaw the power to crush hard foods like nuts and raw vegetables. It is even possible to feel the strong muscles controlling the jaw. To do this, clench the teeth together tightly. Next, hold a hand near the lower jaw and then near the temple above the eyes. What are felt are just a few of the muscles that give the jaw its impressive strength.

The jaw, along with the skeleton, grows from birth until an individual is about twenty years old. A newborn infant has a very small jaw. That is one reason why babies have such soft features and must consume special baby food, which is often pureed or finely chopped. By the time the person is six years old, the lower jaw has greatly increased in size. At twenty, both the upper and lower jaws have fully developed.

The Mouth

Set in between the upper and lower jaws is the mouth, with the lips forming an entrance to the mouth's interior. Glancing in a mirror reveals that the lips do not look like they are covered with the same kind of skin that surrounds the rest of the body. This is because the lips are made from a unique set of muscle fibers and elastic tissue. The fibers and tissue that form the lips are like a cross between regular skin and the membrane, or thin covering, lining the inside of the mouth. Unlike most skin, the lips have no hairs or sweat and oil glands. Glands are organs that secrete, or leak out, certain substances like hormones and saliva.

Taking a look inside the mouth, the top is bound by a part of the upper jaw known as the hard palate. It is hard because the tongue and lower jaw need something to push up against in order to crush food. Resting alongside the hard palate is the soft palate, which extends back

Why It Is Better to Smile

Given its extraordinary flexibility, the mouth is one of the most expressive features of the face. Holding the lips tightly together can show concern or anger. An open mouth indicates surprise. A down-turned mouth suggests sadness, while an upturned, open mouth causes the whole face to lift up into a smile.

Frowning actually requires a lot more energy and effort than smiling. Forty-three muscles are activated with a frown, but only seventeen are required to produce a smile. Smiling, therefore, promotes relaxation and helps to prevent certain wrinkles. It is the world's best face-lift!

into the throat. This tissue, more tender than the hard palate, moves upward when food is swallowed. Without the soft palate, food would shoot up and out of the nose!

A U-shaped piece of tissue hangs in the back center of the mouth from the soft palate. This tissue is called the uvula. Often cartoons show characters yelling with their mouths wide open, revealing the uvula. Its function in the mouth and throat remains somewhat of a mystery, as scientists still are unsure what it does. Many believe it helps to close off air passages coming from the nose, lessening the chances of choking on food.

Underneath the hard and soft palates are the tonsils. These two organs help to remove germs that may enter the throat from food and air. Sometimes the tonsils become infected—most often in children— and must be removed.

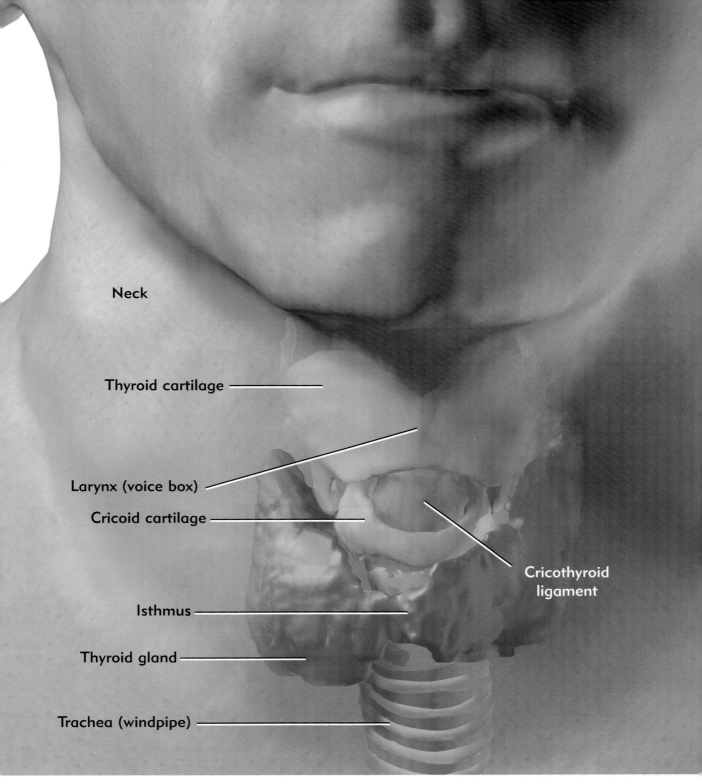

Neck

Thyroid cartilage —————

Larynx (voice box) ——————

Cricoid cartilage ————————

Cricothyroid ligament

Isthmus ————————————

Thyroid gland ———————

Trachea (windpipe) ——————————

This view of the throat shows the trachea, larynx, and thyroid. The thyroid is the gland that controls the body's rate of metabolism and promotes growth during childhood.

The Throat

Leading from the back of the mouth and down into the neck is the throat. It is the area that directs air from the nose to the lungs, and food and liquids from the mouth into the stomach. The throat is divided into two main parts: the pharynx and the larynx.

The pharynx is a muscular passage that extends from the nose to the esophagus, the tubelike structure that sends food to the stomach. About five inches long, the pharynx is the crossroads for movement of air, food, and liquids. Not everything goes down to the stomach, however. Like trains switching tracks, air can be diverted down through the trachea into the lungs.

The trachea, or windpipe, looks a bit like a vacuum-cleaner hose. Just as a hose has plastic for flexibility and support, the trachea has rings of cartilage surrounding it. The cartilage rings prevent the trachea from collapsing and allow for intake of different levels of air. Tiny hairlike appendages called cilia stick out of a slimy membrane lining the trachea. They help to keep the throat clean and ensure that food and water move smoothly.

The trachea has a flap of cartilage above it called the epiglottis. Like a lid, the epiglottis closes the entrance to the windpipe when food is swallowed. Without it, food and liquid could wind up in the lungs instead of the stomach.

Above the trachea are the thyroid glands, which together look like a bow tie in the throat. The thyroid glands control fuel use in the body, calcium levels, and growth. They are protected by a section of cartilage commonly called the Adam's apple, which is the largest of nine sections of cartilage in the larynx, or voice box. This cartilage sticks out like a bump in the throat. The bump is particularly noticeable in men, as they generally have larger larynxes than women.

The Larynx

Before air travels from the nose to the trachea, it must first move across the larynx, a triangular box about 1.6 inches long that opens behind the tongue in the throat. The inside looks like a tube with a slit in the middle lined on both sides with white reedy material. This material forms the vocal cords.

When breathing, the vocal cords open to allow air to flow freely down the trachea. When speaking, the cords draw closer together. Airflow makes the cords vibrate, which produces sound waves. The tightness of the cords determines the rate of vibration and pitch. Larynx size also affects the sound. People with small voice boxes generally have high-pitched voices while large larynxes produce lower tones. That is why men tend to have deeper voices than women.

Frontal sinus

Sphenoid sinus

Superior nasal concha

Middle nasal concha

Inferior nasal concha

Nasal cavity

Soft palate

Epiglottis cartilage

Epiglottis

Hyoid bone

Vocal cords

Trachea (windpipe)

This is a cross-sectional view of the mouth and nose. The epiglottis closes the passage to the windpipe when we eat or drink so that food and liquids don't enter our lungs.

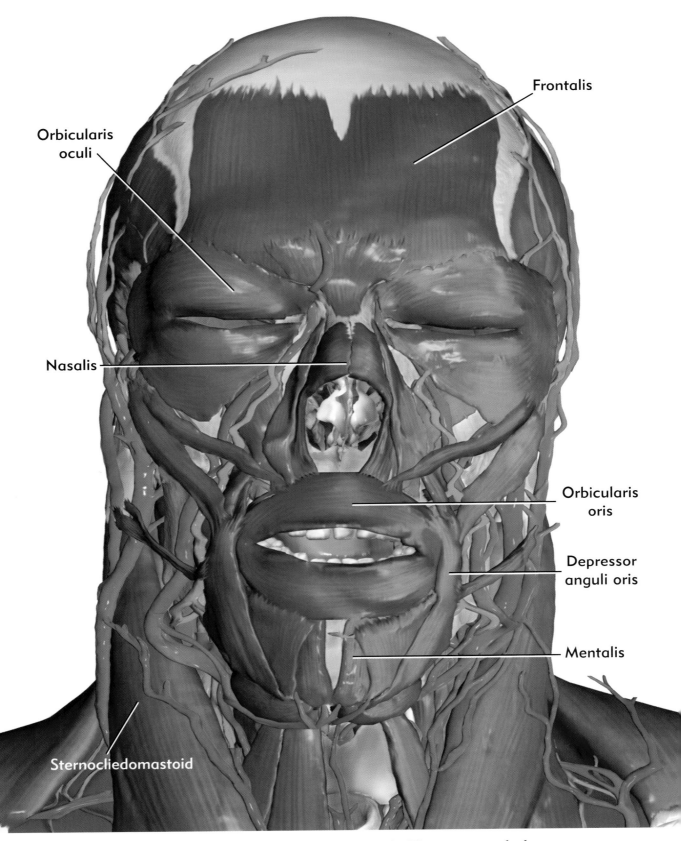

Frontalis

Orbicularis oculi

Nasalis

Orbicularis oris

Depressor anguli oris

Mentalis

Sternocliedomastoid

These are the muscles of the head and neck. They control the movements of the jaw, and they also control the way our faces express emotion.

14

2
EATING

Humans must eat food to fuel the body. Food provides energy that drives virtually all activities, from basic functions like the heart beating to high-energy movements such as running. The more active a person is, the more energy, or food, he or she requires.

The human body, however, is much more sophisticated than a car. Food not only gives energy, but it also provides nutrients that promote the body's ability to grow and maintain itself. These nutrients include proteins, carbohydrates, fats, oils, minerals, and vitamins. Different foods contain varying amounts of these nutrients, which is why it is important to eat a balanced diet. Nuts, for example, are high in protein, while vegetables are high in fiber, minerals, and vitamins.

Food cannot enter the stomach as is. Imagine swallowing a whole banana. It must first be chewed into a manageable pulp. In addition to the jaw muscles, muscles all around the face, including those in the lips and cheeks, control chewing. The lip and cheek muscles primarily hold the food in place so that the teeth can do their job.

Teeth

Teeth may seem like hard, lifeless objects, but they are very much alive. These bonelike structures are attached to the jaws as though they were plants growing out of soil. Teeth have two main jobs. First, they bite into food and chop it into pieces that can be managed in the mouth. Second, teeth crush, munch, and pulverize food into a mashed-up pulp that can be swallowed.

When a child begins to lose baby teeth, this marks the development of permanent teeth. Before that time, individuals have what are known as milk teeth. Milk teeth cells begin to form in the womb, before a baby is born. At birth, young infants possess thick gum pads, which contain the cells necessary for teeth development. When the baby reaches about six months of age, teeth begin to erupt. Their emergence continues until about the age of two, when the child usually has a full set of twenty milk teeth. After the age of six, the milk teeth begin to fall out and are replaced by permanent teeth. By the age of twenty, most people should have a set of thirty-two teeth, if wisdom teeth and other teeth are not removed or accidentally knocked out.

There are four types of permanent teeth: incisors, canines (also called eyeteeth), premolars, and molars. Incise means to cut, and that is what incisors do. These have a narrow edge shaped like a knife blade. Incisors cut or bite into food and chop it into small pieces. To see what they look like, smile and look in a mirror at the front teeth. These are incisors.

Canine teeth are located to the sides of the incisors. They rip and tear food apart. Think of biting into a chewy piece of bread or meat. The mouth opens wider to expose the canines so they can tear off bite-sized morsels. While incisors have a flat edge on the bottom, canines are pointed. This can be felt by running the tongue over them.

Premolars are like a cross between a canine and a molar. They have slightly more jagged edges than canines. The main job of premolars is to cut and chew. Usually this action is done to pieces of food bitten off by the incisors and canines.

Molars have a wide exposed surface area that enables them to chew and crush. Given their shape and location at the back of the gum line, molars are not effective at cutting and biting. They grind food that has already been cut up by the other teeth. Wisdom teeth are molars that erupt in 75 percent of people by the time they reach the age of eighteen.

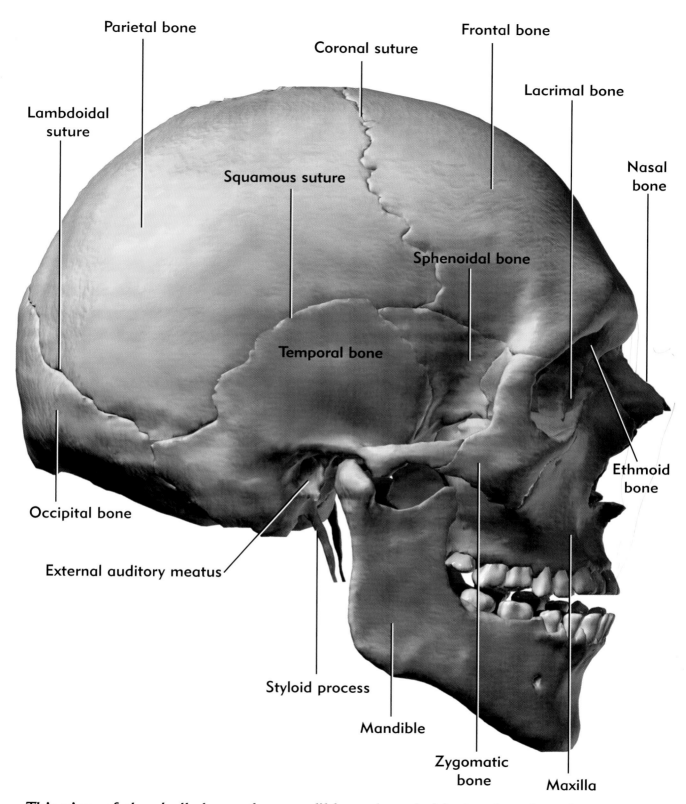

Parietal bone

Coronal suture

Frontal bone

Lacrimal bone

Nasal bone

Lambdoidal suture

Squamous suture

Sphenoidal bone

Temporal bone

Ethmoid bone

Occipital bone

External auditory meatus

Styloid process

Mandible

Zygomatic bone

Maxilla

This view of the skull shows the mandible and teeth. Notice that there is no bone structure for the lower nose, which is formed entirely from cartilage.

Flossing

Toothbrushes often miss the tight areas between teeth, so it is also important to floss daily. Waxed and unwaxed dental flosses are available. Both work well when used properly.

To floss, wind an eighteen-inch piece of floss around the middle fingers of each hand. Using the thumbs and forefingers, slide the floss between each tooth, gently scraping any plaque off the tooth sides. Repeat with a clean section of floss for each area in the mouth. After flossing, rinse the mouth thoroughly with water or mouthwash.

A throwback to earlier stages in human evolutionary development, wisdom teeth often do not fit properly in the jaw, which has gotten smaller among all people over time. In such cases, the wisdom teeth must be extracted. If possible, visit a museum with skeleton models of early human ancestors to see how big their jaws and mouths were.

Inside a Tooth

Like humans, teeth come in different shapes and sizes on the outside. On the inside, however, they essentially are the same. Each tooth consists of two main parts: the crown and the root. The crown is the portion of the tooth that is visible in the mouth. The root is the part that is embedded within the jaw. When a tooth falls out or is extracted, the root can be seen as a pointy, hard tip on the bottom of the tooth.

A cross-section diagram reveals that teeth are composed of layers. The outer layer consists of enamel, a hard substance that protects the tooth. Underneath the enamel is dentin, a softer material. In the center of every tooth, there is a pulp cavity containing nerves and blood vessels.

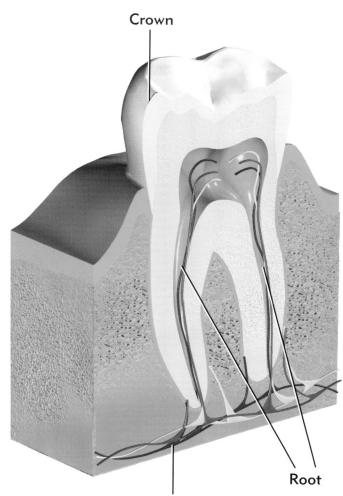

Crown

Root

Nerves and blood vessels

This is a cross section of the interior of a tooth, showing the root and nerve structure, as well as the blood vessels.

Finally, a material called cementum glues the tooth in place within the jawbone.

With all of their nooks and crannies, teeth can contain bacteria from food. Over time, this leads to plaque, a combination of rotting food, bacteria, and other tooth-decaying substances. If the bacteria are not removed by brushing, they can produce acids that may eat through the enamel and into the dentin. The resulting damage can create cavities. Dentists fill cavities because the infection could spread to the pulp, then into the jawbone, where it could lead to blood poisoning. It is, therefore, very important to brush the teeth after every meal and to visit a dentist regularly.

What Happens to Food

The mouth is the entryway for the body's digestive system. When food or liquid enters the mouth, it begins a journey that can extend over twenty feet. Food is first chewed into a ball called a bolus. The tongue pushes the bolus toward the back of the pharynx. When the ball of food touches the throat, a series of reactions occur that induce swallowing.

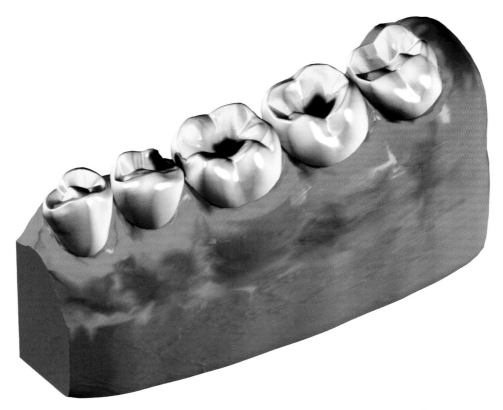

This image illustrates some molars with filled cavities. The molars are large teeth in the back of the mouth used for grinding food.

As the throat muscles push food downward, the soft palate moves upward to prevent the bolus from going up the nose. The epiglottis then seals the trachea closed. Sometimes, the lidlike epiglottis does not close fast enough, often when a person is eating and talking at the same time, which can cause a choking sensation because food or liquid has entered the lungs.

Usually, however, the epiglottis does its job correctly, and food is sent down the esophagus. Try placing the fingers of one hand on either side of the top of the throat while swallowing. Notice how swallowing is not as simple as pouring water down a drain, but instead requires several movements. Muscle contractions, known as peristalsis, push the food in waves to the stomach. Thanks to peristalsis, a person could eat sitting sideways or upside down, and the food would still get to the stomach.

The stomach showers its contents with digestive juices that break the food down into a liquefied pulp. The pulp then travels through the small and large intestines. Part of the small intestine, called the jejunum, allows the nutrients in the food to pass into the blood, which carries the nutrients throughout the entire body.

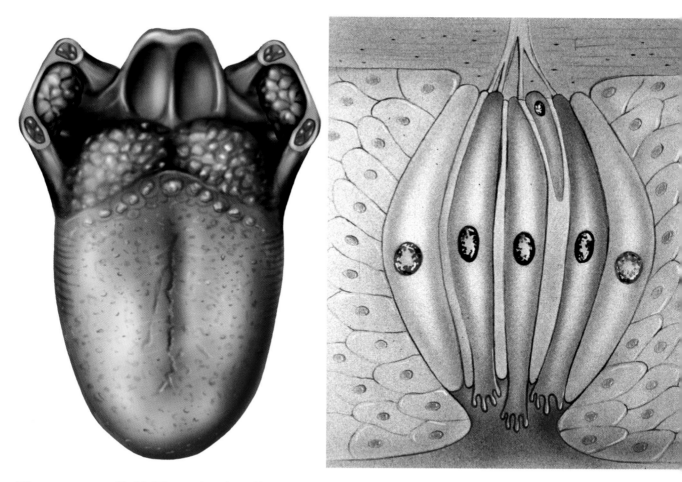

The tongue *(left)*. Taste bud cells *(right)*. Taste buds sense sweet, sour, salty, and bitter foods, and the nose helps us taste what we eat.

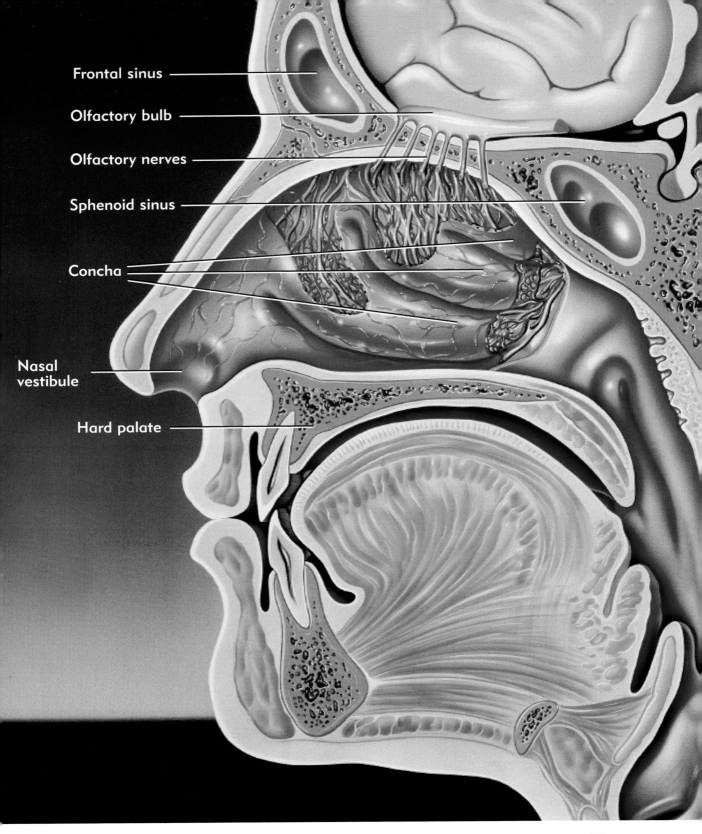

Frontal sinus

Olfactory bulb

Olfactory nerves

Sphenoid sinus

Concha

Nasal vestibule

Hard palate

This cross section of the head illustrates the structure of the nose. The olfactory nerves extend down into the nasal cavity from the olfactory bulb.

3
THE NOSE

The nose is perhaps the world's best air conditioner. It not only takes in air and expels gaseous waste, but it also filters out irritants, such as dust and dirt. The nose then warms and moistens air so that it can circulate properly to the lungs and then to the rest of the body. Mechanical air conditioners require constant external maintenance and repair, but the nose is a self-sufficient powerhouse that continues to work throughout a healthy person's lifetime.

The exterior part of the nose gains its shape and structure from bone and cartilage. Cartilage gives the nose a certain amount of flexibility, while bones attach the nose to the skull. One area of attachment can be felt by placing the thumb and forefinger at the bridge of the nose near the eyes.

Inside, the nose is divided into two narrow sections called the nasal fossae. The divider is called the septum. Like the outside of the nose, the septum is made from bone and cartilage. It is covered with a delicate lining referred to as the mucous membrane. This membrane helps to keep the nose warm and moist. Lining the nostrils are several tiny strong hairs. These hairs protect the entrance of the nose and help to filter out large particles.

The Nasal Conchae

Behind the fossae is a bone divided into three parts by ridges. Together the ridges are called the nasal conchae. They look like three slides because they rise near the brain region and then slope downward before dividing into the fossae. Between each concha—the singular for conchae—is a passage called the meatus (pronounced mee-aye-tuss). As with the septum, the meatus is lined with a mucous membrane, except this membrane has a very rich blood supply. As a result, and because of its structure, the meatus is active in warming and moistening air that is breathed in from the nose. Mucus helps in this process.

Most people think of mucus as a disgusting substance that only occurs with a cold. Actually, the meatuses in an average person secrete nearly a pint of mucus each day. Look at a pint of milk in the grocery store to get an idea of how much is made. This slimy substance is like an air cleaning fluid. It flows over cilia on the meatuses and enables them to trap dust and other undesirable things in air. The cilia move the waste material, collected in mucus, out of the nose region and into the throat where they can be swallowed and then disposed of by the body.

The Sinuses

There are eight holes, or sinuses, in the head. They are located between the eyes and nose, behind the eyebrows, and in back of the cheeks. They produce mucus when the nose does not make enough. They also help to give the face some resistance to impacts, such as punches to the head or falls on a hard surface. The sinuses decrease the weight of nasal bones. They also give resonance, or an appealing vibration and tone, to the voice. Individuals with beautiful singing voices often owe much of their natural talent to the shape and structure of their sinuses, along with the flexibility of the vocal cords.

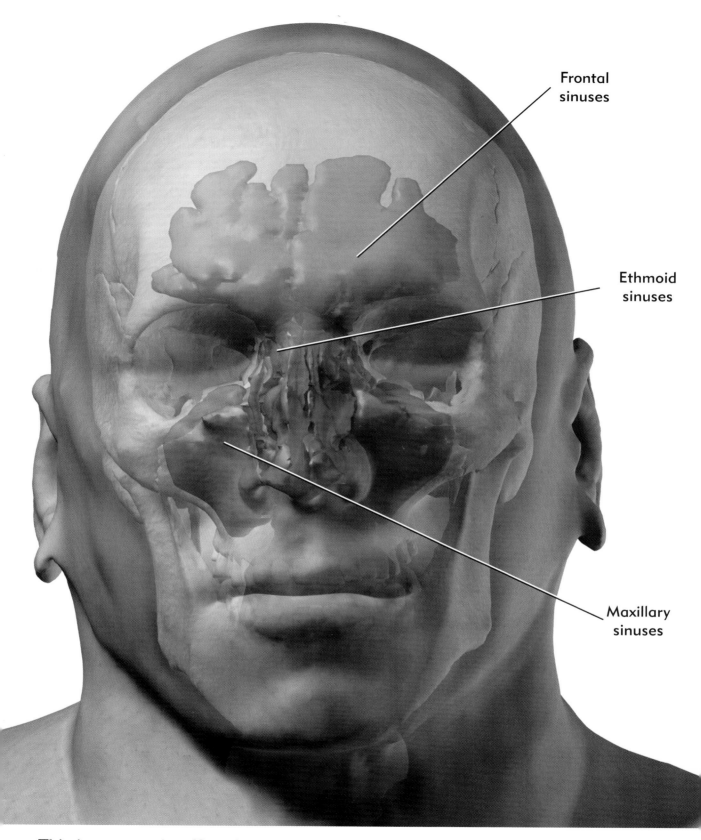

Frontal
sinuses

Ethmoid
sinuses

Maxillary
sinuses

This is an anterior (front) view of the nasal cavities. The sinus cavities help
to warm and moisten air before it reaches the lungs.

What Happens During a Sneeze

Sneezes help to rid the lungs and nose of irritants, such as pollen, dust, or germs. One or more of these irritants may settle on the mucous membrane in the nose. When this happens, nerves immediately send a signal to the breathing muscles, which begin a sneeze.

First, the individual takes a sudden deep breath, causing the lungs to expand. The airways then burst open, the eyes close, and the lungs shoot out their contents through the mouth and nose, likely forcing the irritant out of the body.

The Ear, Eye, Nose, and Throat Connection

The meatuses branch off into ducts and tubes leading to the eyes and ears. Tear ducts, for example, carry tears—made of a saltwater solution that protects the eyeball—away from the eyes, past the nose and down into the throat. That is why people often have to blow their noses during, or after, crying.

Since the nose and ears both lead to the throat, the activities of the nose can affect the ears. Blowing the nose too hard can rupture the eardrum. It may also send germs in nose mucus into the sinuses near the ears, which could cause an ear infection.

The mouth is connected to the ears via the throat. For example, chewing gum often relieves pressure on the ears when flying or making a sudden descent in an airplane. That is because the chewing sensation may cause the connection between the ear and the throat—the eustachian tube—to open and release air. The eustachian tube normally can do this on its own, but sometimes quick changes in pressure cause it to retain air and create a popping sensation in the ear.

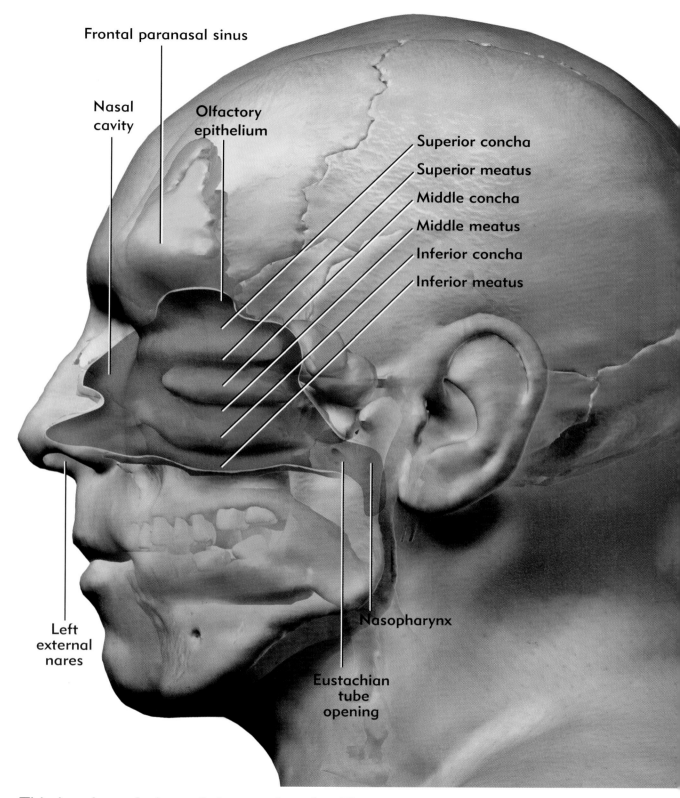

Frontal paranasal sinus

Nasal cavity

Olfactory epithelium

Superior concha

Superior meatus

Middle concha

Middle meatus

Inferior concha

Inferior meatus

Left external nares

Nasopharynx

Eustachian tube opening

This is a lateral view of the nasal cavity. The meatus passageways are lined with mucous membranes. Mucus traps dust and dirt particles and cleans the air going to the lungs.

Breathing

At rest, most people breathe about twelve times a minute. During strenuous exercise, the breathing rate can increase to eighty times per minute. In fact, every day each individual breathes in and out 5,000 gallons of air. People even breathe while sleeping. Snoring, by the way, can occur when a person breathes through the mouth while sleeping, which is often the result of a partial blockage of the nose and throat. The uvula at the back of the mouth vibrates, causing the snoring sound.

Breathing is part of a process known as respiration. The purpose of respiration is to supply the body with oxygen, which helps to release energy and to burn food. Oxygen is essential to human life. While people can go without food for a day or so, it would be impossible to exist without oxygen.

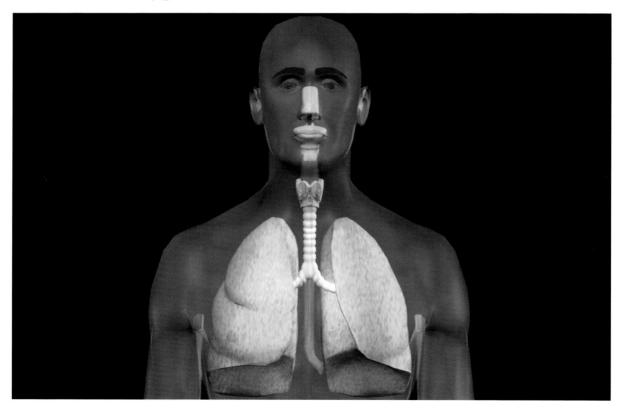

The trachea, or windpipe, connects to the lungs. People can breathe through either the nose or mouth, but breathing through the nose is healthier.

Respiration also involves the release of carbon dioxide, which is a waste product of certain processes within the body. Oxygen is breathed in and carbon dioxide is exhaled. Respiration is normally an involuntary activity, meaning that people do not have to consciously think about breathing in order for it to happen. However, it is possible to control breathing. For example, think of taking a deep breath before swimming or blowing up a balloon.

The oxygen inhaled from the nose travels down the trachea and into the lungs. A muscle below the lungs called the diaphragm performs most of this work. It can be felt going up and down with each breath. Capillaries, or tiny blood vessels, surround the lungs. They transport the oxygen to blood. Like a car that has just been filled with gasoline, the oxygenated blood is then transported to the heart, which pumps the energized blood throughout the body. Exhaling is the opposite of inhaling. The blood transports carbon dioxide to the lungs. The lungs send the carbon dioxide up through the trachea and throat where it can be released through the nose or mouth.

Although it is possible to breathe through the mouth, it is much better to do so through the nose, since the nose can filter out unwanted dust and germs. There are times, however, when a huge gust of air is desired. That is one reason why people sometimes breathe through the mouth after strenuous activity.

Breathing can become difficult when the inside of the nose and the sinuses become inflamed, or swollen with mucus. Germs are not the only culprits. Many people are allergic to certain pollens and molds. When inhaled, these cause allergy victims to produce protective agents called histamines. These increase mucus production and help to rid the body of airborne irritants. That is why people with allergies wheeze and sneeze a lot. Antihistamine drugs provide some relief, but the best prevention is to avoid breathing the irritant in the first place by staying indoors.

Taste buds with papillae. There are thousands of taste buds on the upper surface of the tongue. Without them, food would seem to have no flavor.

4
THE SENSES OF TASTE AND SMELL

Humans possess five senses that connect them to the outside world: smell, taste, sight, touch, and hearing. The mouth and nose are responsible for tasting and smelling. The sense of taste is the least developed of all five senses, meaning that it provides less information about the external world than sight, smell, touch, and hearing. Still, taste does help to identify food and makes life a lot more fun.

The Tongue

Stick out your tongue in front of a mirror. Based on what is visible, the tongue looks sort of like a shoe sole. There is, however, more to the tongue than meets the eye. The tongue actually fills most of the lower part of the mouth above the mandible. It also extends into the front of the throat because it is attached to the epiglottis. While people may pride themselves on their arm or leg muscles, the tongue is one of the most active and mobile muscles in the body. It can move up and down, from side to side, and in circles, and it can even curl up on itself.

Just as teeth are rooted in the lower jaw, so is the tongue. It is attached by two muscles—the geniohyoid and mylohyoid—and a bone called the hyoid. The hyoid bone, which sort of looks like a boomerang, is fixed just below the epiglottis. The job of the mouth muscles, including the tongue itself, is to move and process food. Taste buds on the surface of the tongue inform the individual about what he or she is eating or drinking.

Taste Buds

It is a misconception that the visible bumps on the tongue are individual taste buds. These tiny projections are called papillae. Between each papilla are tiny spaces, or ridges. The spaces form mini-moats around the papillae. Food and liquid roll off the papillae and seep down into the ridges, where many taste buds are located. Taste buds also are present on the palates and on the inside of the throat.

Taste buds are made out of tiny receptor cells. Each cell has a small hairlike projection sticking out of it. These projections are called microvilli. Food coming into contact with the receptor cells sends a message to the brain through a network of nerve fibers. Since each person has about 9,000 to 10,000 taste buds, this process could get confusing, but all of the impulses channel into two main nerve bundles.

It is amazing to think that taste buds respond to only four basic tastes: sweet, salty, sour, and bitter. Think of how many different foods are consumed and how unique each tastes. The unique flavor of each food comes from varying combinations of the four basic tastes, along with the food's texture, smell, and other qualities.

While researchers are still analyzing how the taste buds pick up individual flavors, it is generally thought that buds at the tip of the tongue respond to sweet tastes. The sides of the tongue, just behind the tip, are believed to detect salty flavors. Sour tastes are picked up behind the salty detectors. Bitter flavors are identified toward the back center of the tongue. It is interesting that the tongue is 8,000 times more sensitive to bitter tastes than it is to sweet ones. That is

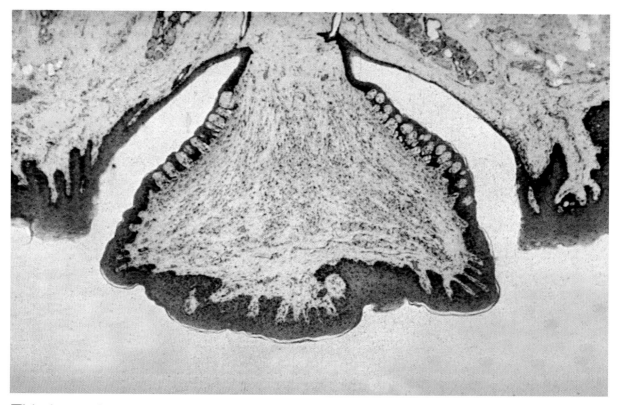

**This is a microscopic image of a cross section of a taste bud.
Each taste bud is a nerve fiber that sends messages to the brain.**

why bitter medicine often is flavored with a sweetener. The sweetness makes the medicine more palatable, or pleasing to the taste buds on the tongue and palate.

Some foods do not get their flavor from the taste buds. Hot chiles or other spicy foods gain most of their punch by stimulating nerves on the tongue that are sensitive to pain. It can be a pleasant sensation, though, particularly for people who are used to the stimulating jolt.

Saliva

Since food must travel into the moatlike depressions between papillae to reach most of the taste buds, food must be suspended in a liquid. As many foods are quite dry, saliva provides the necessary liquid. For example, swallow all of the saliva in your mouth. Next,

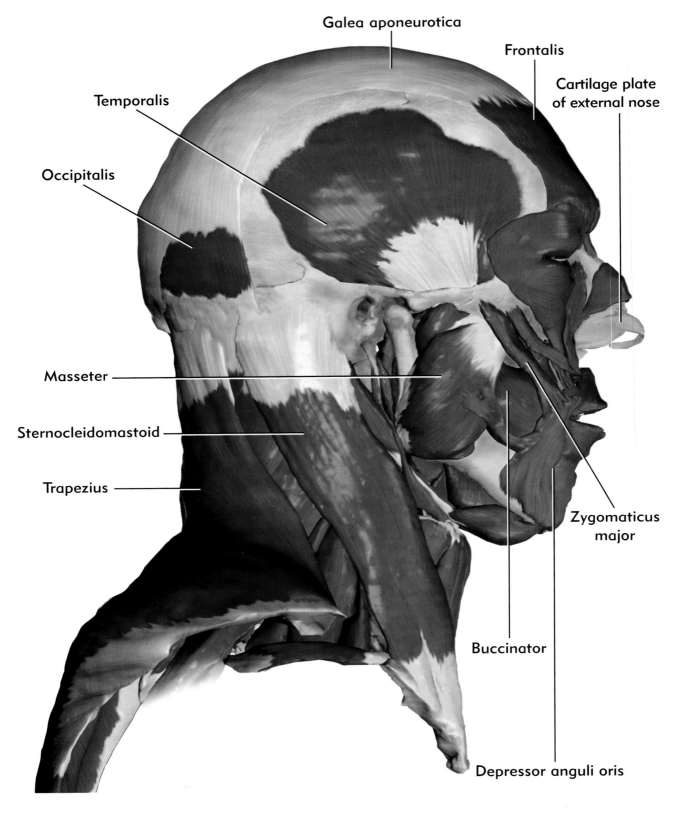

Galea aponeurotica

Frontalis

Cartilage plate
of external nose

Temporalis

Occipitalis

Masseter

Sternocleidomastoid

Trapezius

Zygomaticus
major

Buccinator

Depressor anguli oris

The temporalis and masseter are two powerful muscles that pull the jaw closed during chewing. The buccinator muscle pulls the cheeks inward during sucking.

place a small piece of bread or cereal on the tongue. Hold it there for a few seconds and see if it has much flavor. Saliva also helps to digest, or break down, foods and liquids before they enter the stomach.

Saliva is produced twenty-four hours a day. In fact, each day the average person makes about three pints of saliva. Saliva contains four main ingredients: water, mucus, ptyalin, and lysozyme. Ptyalin is an enzyme, or a substance that aids in digesting food. Lysozyme is an antiseptic chemical that prevents infections from forming in the mouth. Saliva, therefore, acts a bit like an antibacterial soap in the mouth.

Three pairs of glands produce and secrete saliva. Each set creates a different mixture that, when combined together, make saliva. For example, the parotids, which are located in the neck near the jaw and ear, create a watery solution with lots of ptyalin. The sublingual glands, however, make a thick, mucus-filled saliva. Small tubes, or ducts, connect the glands.

Why Animals and Insects Are Better Smellers

Pet owners know that if a treat is hidden in an out-of-the-way place, the pet can usually sniff around and find it. That is because animals and insects generally are better than humans at detecting odors.

When humans smell, the odor must travel to the inside of the nose before it can be processed. Animals and insects identify odors more directly. A dog, for example, has smell receptors near the tip of its nose. In addition, the dog's smell receptor sites are 100 times larger than those of humans.

Smell

The sense of smell is much more powerful than the sense of taste. It would take about 25,000 times more of something to be tasted instead of smelled. Although not always obvious, smelling provides us with a constant source of information about the outside world. It warns of dangers, as when smelling smoke from a fire. On a subconscious level, it even contributes to being attracted to another person. The sense of smell also greatly adds to taste. For example, a blindfolded person with his or her nose plugged would have a hard time tasting the difference between a slice of raw potato and a slice of apple. The smell of these foods, however, allows for easy identification.

Olfactory Area

Smelling occurs above the nasal conchae in a region just under the brain known as the olfactory area. This area is packed with millions of small cells. Like taste buds, each olfactory cell possesses a hairlike projection. In this case, the projections are called cilia. Mucus surrounds the cilia to help trap odors and to keep the hairy objects moist. Moisture is essential because gaseous substances and wetness heighten smell. Gasoline, for example, gives off almost chokingly strong fumes, while a teaspoon of dry salt is nearly odorless.

It is thought that individual components of odors dissolve in the mucus and then stick on the cilia. The cilia then send electrical signals to the brain through a segmented piece of bone called the ethmoidal. The brain processes the various signals and identifies what is being smelled.

Because the olfactory area is close to the region of the brain associated with emotions, mood, and memory, smells can affect feelings.

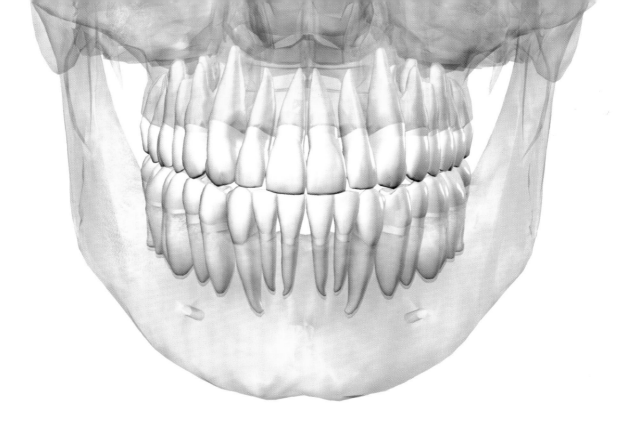

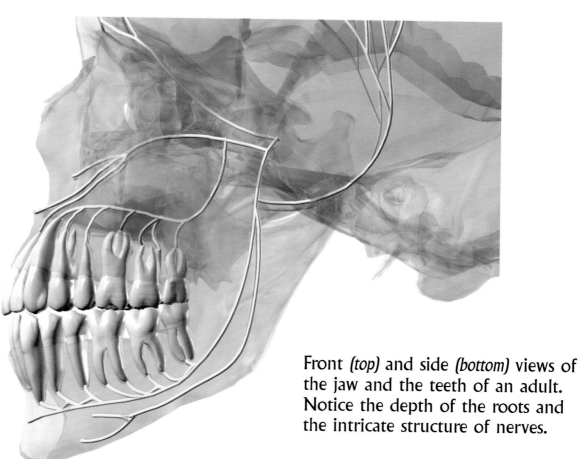

Front *(top)* and side *(bottom)* views of
the jaw and the teeth of an adult.
Notice the depth of the roots and
the intricate structure of nerves.

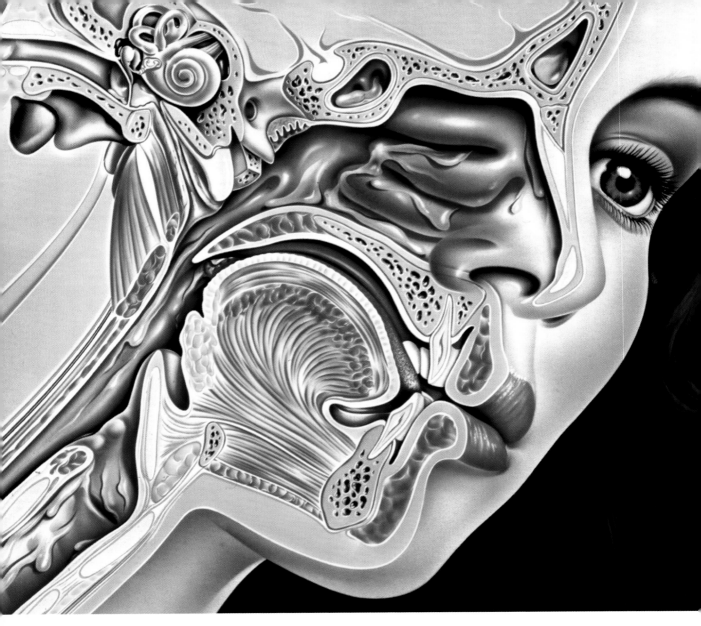

A cutaway illustration of the mouth, nose, and ear. Note the secretion of mucus inside the nose. Mucus helps to warm the air going to the lungs and removes dust particles.

Smelling a favorite food makes the mouth water and creates a mental picture of what that food tastes like even before it goes into the mouth. As people get older, they collect greater numbers of these smell memories. The odors in the area where you are currently reading this book, therefore, may one day bring back memories of learning about the nose, the mouth, and the senses of smell and taste.

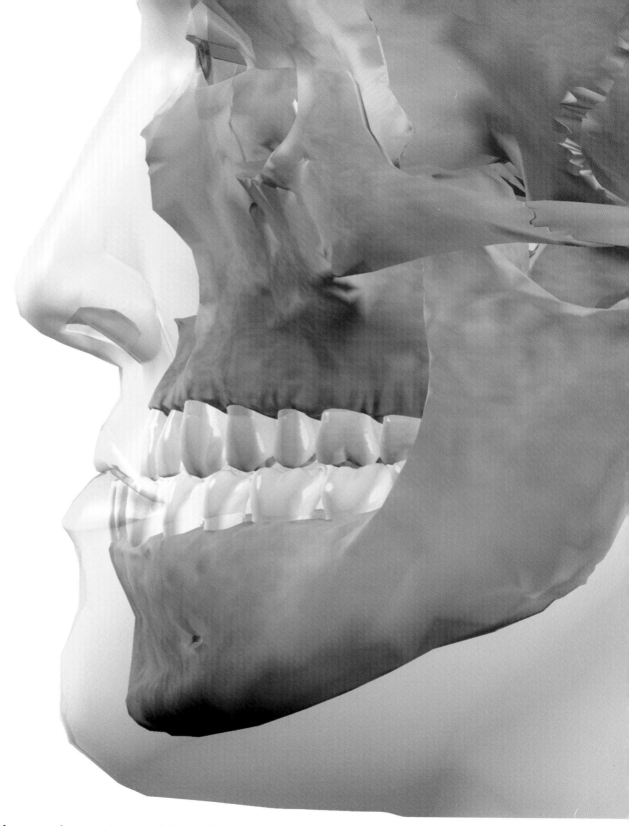

This image shows the position of the bones of the mouth and nose within the head. The shape of the skull determines what the facial features look like.

GLOSSARY

carbon dioxide Waste product of breathing. It is exhaled through the lungs and out of the nose.

cilia Small, hairlike structures, such as those within the nose and throat.

digestion Process of breaking down food into smaller components that can be absorbed into the bloodstream.

epiglottis Lidlike piece of cartilage that closes off the windpipe when anything is swallowed.

esophagus Passageway that enables food to travel from the mouth to the stomach.

gland Organ that produces a substance required by the body. For example, salivary glands make saliva.

larynx Triangular box that opens behind the tongue in the throat. It contains the vocal cords.

mandible Hinged lower part of the jaw that moves up and down to control chewing.

maxilla Upper part of the jaw.

mucous membrane Thin sheet of tissue covered with mucus, a protective slimy substance.

nasal fossae Two narrow channels in the front part of the nose.

palate Roof of the mouth that consists of both hard and soft parts. It separates the mouth from the nose.

peristalsis Muscle contractions that send food from the throat to the stomach.

pharynx Muscular passage extending from the nose to the esophagus that allows for the movement of air, food, and liquids.

saliva Liquid containing water, mucus, and an enzyme called ptyalin that helps to break down food, and a chemical called lysozyme that has antiseptic, or germ killing, properties.

septum Divider, made of bone and cartilage, that separates the nasal fossae.

sinuses Cavities, or holes, in the skull that help to lessen the impact of blows to the face and also, when necessary, help to produce mucus.

taste buds   Structures located in the mouth, on the tongue, and in the throat that help to identify flavors.

trachea   Tube that enables air to travel from the throat to the lungs; also called the windpipe.

uvula   U-shaped appendage attached to the soft palate that helps to close off nasal air passages when swallowing to prevent choking.

vocal cords   Two reedlike white folds of tissue in the larynx that can move, stretch, and vibrate to produce different sounds.

FOR MORE INFORMATION

Magazines

Kids Discover

This publication covers science topics for youths six years and older.

Multimedia

Interactive Human Body

Mega Systems/Glasklar Interactive

Web site: http://www.glasklar.com/us/index.shtml

This CD-ROM features a multidimensional tour of the human body.

Ultimate 3D Skeleton: School Version

Dorling Kindersley Multimedia

Web site: http://www.dk.com

This CD-ROM enables students to explore each of the 206 bones in the human body in 3-D format.

Web Sites

American Lung Association
http://www.lungusa.org/school

KidSource Online
http://www.kidsource.com/kidsource/pages/Health.html
This site provides links to virtual activities, information, and other Web sites.

National Institutes of Health
http://www.nih.gov

National Library of Medicine
http://www.nlm.nih.gov

The Online Medical Dictionary
http://www.graylab.ac.uk/omd

FOR FURTHER READING

Silverstein, Alvin. *Human Body Systems Series*. Brookfield, MA: Twenty-First Century Books, 1994.

Stangl, Jean. *What Makes You Cough, Sneeze, Burp, Hiccup, Blink, Yawn, Sweat, and Shiver?* New York: Franklin Watts Inc., 2000.

Suzuki, David, and Barbara Hehner. *Looking at Senses.* New York: John Wiley & Sons, 1991.

Swanson, Diane. *Burp! The Most Interesting Book You'll Ever Read About Eating*. Tonawanda, NY: Kids Can Press, 2001.

Treays, Rebecca. *Understanding Your Senses.* San Jose, CA: EDC Publications, 1998.

Tytla, Milan. *Come to Your Senses (All Eleven of Them)*. Toronto: Annick Press Limited, 1993.

Wiese, Jim. *Head to Toe Science: Over 40 Eye-Popping, Spine-Tingling, Heart-Pounding Activities That Teach Kids About the Human Body.* New York: John Wiley & Sons, 2000.

INDEX

About the Author

Jennifer Viegas is a reporter for *Discovery Channel Online News* and is a feature columnist for Knight Ridder newspapers. She has worked as a journalist for ABC News, PBS, and other media. Jennifer also helped to write two cookbooks for *Cooking Light*.

Photo Credits

Cover, pp. 1, 4, 7, 8, 11, 13, 14, 17, 25, 27, 34 © Visible Productions, by arrangement with Anatographica, LLC; pp. 19, 20, 28, 37, 39 © Williams & Wilkins, A Waverly Company; pp. 21, 30, 33 © CMSP; pp. 22, 38 © Photo Researchers.

Series Design

Claudia Carlson

Layout

Nelson Sá